Simply Knitted With Love

12 hand knitted projects and simple recipes for you, your home and as gifts

Daniella Taylor and Linda Williams

quail studio

Published in 2015 by
Quail Publishing
1/4 Black Horse Barns
Fancott
Toddington
Bedfordshire, LU5 6HT
UK

Jolie, 80 High St, Walkern,
Stevenage, SG2 7PG
www.jolie-home.co.uk
01438 861717

ISBN: 978-0-9927707-6-1

Conceived, designed and produced by

q u a i l s t u d i o

Art Editor: Georgina Brant
Graphic Design: Quail Studio
Technical Editor: Kate Heppell
Photography: Jesse Wild
Creative Director: Darren Brant
Yarn Support: Rowan Yarns
Designer: Jolie;
Daniella Taylor & Linda Williams

Printed in the UK

British Library Cataloguing in Publication Data
A catalogue record for this book is available from the British Library

@quail_studio
@joliehome

Simply Knitted With Love

12 hand knitted projects and simple recipes for you, your home and as gifts

From wraps and throws to snoods and hats, we've compiled our favourite patterns from over ten years of Jolie designs. Many of them are simple yet effective projects especially suitable for the beginner, but we've also included some more challenging ones for the progressing or more experienced knitter.

Whether you fancy a little, well-earned, self indulgence by knitting for yourself, or wish to create that extra special gift for a loved one, these projects will bring years of pleasure, comfort and admiration.

Opened in May 2005, Jolie is a haven of creativity, inspiration and friendship, where our weekly Knit & Chat groups draw loyal and new customers from miles around to share ideas on knitting, crocheting, recipes and just about anything to help make life more pleasurable. Indeed, following numerous requests, we're including Linda's mouth-watering cheese scone recipe and some other food favourites. So you can indulge more senses than one!

Dany & Linda

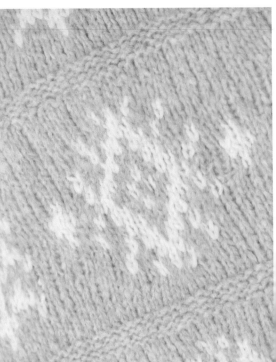

Chamonix Cushion

ROWAN BRUSHED FLEECE

Chamonix Cushion

Cuddle up and relax with this softest of soft cushions.

TENSION
14 sts and 17 rows to 10cm measured over patt on 5mm (US7) needles

SIZE
45cmx45cm

INSTRUCTIONS
Using 5mm (US 7) needles and yarn A, cast on 65 sts.
Work in st st until work measures 24cm, finishing after a WS (purl) row.
Next row (RS): Purl.
Next row: Knit.
Rep these two rows once more.
These four rows create the fold at the base of the cushion.
Next Row (RS): Knit.
Next Row: Purl.
These two rows re-establish st st.
Beginning with RS facing, using the intarsia method, work 22 rows of chart A.
Work a further two rows st st.
Next Row (RS): Purl.
Next Row: Knit.
Rep these two rows once more.
Work two rows st st.

YOU WILL NEED;

YARN
Rowan Brushed Fleece
A Crag 253 (grey version) or Moss 265 (blue version)
3 x 50g
B Cove 251
1 x 50g

NEEDLES
1 pair 5mm (No 6) (US 7) needles

1 pair 8mm (No 0) (US 11) needles (used for casting off only)

OTHER MATERIALS
50 x 50cm cushion pad
5 large press studs

With RS facing, using the intarsia method,
work 22 rows of chart B.
Work a further two rows st st.
Next Row (RS): Purl.
Next Row: Knit.
Repeat these two rows once more.
With RS facing, using the intarsia method,
work 22 rows of chart A.
Work a further two rows st st.
Next Row (RS): Purl.
Next Row: Knit.
Rep these two rows once more.
These four rows create the fold at the
top of the cushion.
Continue in st st until work measures
26cm from top fold.
Cast off using 8mm (US 11) needles.

FINISHING
Using reverse st st top and bottom fold
lines as a guide, pin and sew sides seams
to meet in the middle allowing the top
flap to cover the bottom flap by 2cm.
Position and sew press studs evenly along
opening of cushion back to fasten.

Key
MC
CC

Chart A

Chart B

Frosty Skater Hat

ROWAN ALPACA CHUNKY &
ROWAN KIDSILK HAZE

Frosty Skater Hat

Keep warm and glamorous from the top down with by adding some sparkle and a fun fur pom pom.

TENSION
12 sts and 15 rows to 10cm measured over K2, P2 rib (unstretched) on 9mm (US 13) needles

MEASUREMENTS
Circumference: 50cm (unstretched)
Height: 21cm (excluding pompom)

INSTRUCTIONS
Using 9mm (US 13) needles and with A, B and C held together, cast on 62 sts.

Row 1: *K2, P2, rep from * to last 2 sts, K2.
Row 2: *P2, K2, rep from * to last 2 sts, P2.
Repeat these 2 rows until work measures approx 21cm ending after a WS row.
Next Row (dec row, RS): K2, *p2tog, K2, rep from * to end. 47sts.

FINISHING
Leaving a long tail, break yarns.
Using a large eyed needle and tail yarns, thread through remains stitches on knitting needle. Draw up and secure. Sew up back seam using mattress stitch.

Attach BonPom securely.

YOU WILL NEED;

YARN
A Rowan Alpaca Chunky Wren 072 (grey version) or Dove 070 (white version)
1 x 100g

B Rowan Kidsilk Haze Steel 664 (grey version) or White 612 (white version)
1 x 25g

C Anchor Artiste Metallic Silver 301
1 x 25g

NEEDLES
1 pair 9mm (No 00) (US 13) needles

OTHER MATERIALS
Twilleys Faux Fur Bonpom, Polar 001

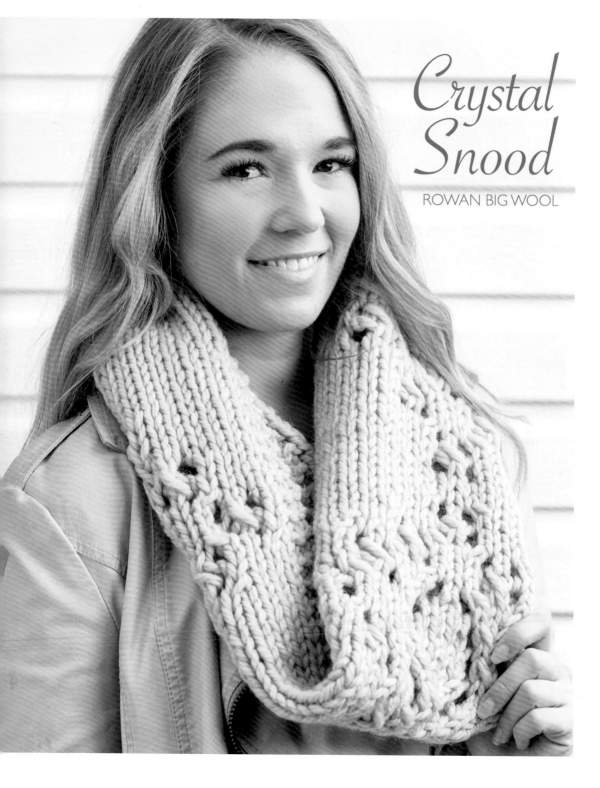

Crystal Snood

ROWAN BIG WOOL

Crystal Snood

Big and bold, slouchy diamond inspired snood.

YOU WILL NEED;

YARN
Rowan Big Wool
Ice Blue 021 or Concrete 061
2 x 100g

NEEDLES
1 pair 12mm (US 17) needles

OTHER SUPPLIES
Large-eyed wool needle

TENSION
8 sts and 12 rows to 10cm measured over st st on 12mm (US 17) needles

SIZE
Circumference: 96cm
Depth: 36cm

INSTRUCTIONS
Using 12mm (US 17) needles, cast on 29 sts.
Work lace pattern from chart or written instructions below.
Row 1: Knit
Row 2 and all WS rows: K3, p23, K3.
Row 3: K12, k2tog, yfwd, K1, yfwd, sl1, K1, psso, K12.
Row 5: K13, yfwd, sl1, k2tog, psso, yfwd, K13.
Row 7: K9, k2tog, yfwd, K1, yfwd, sl1, K1, psso, K1, k2tog, yfwd, K1, yfwd, sl1, K1, psso, k9.
Row 9: K10, yfwd, sl1, k2tog, psso, yfwd, K3, yfwd, sl1, k2tog, psso, yfwd, K10.
Row 11: K6, k2tog, (yfwd, K1, yfwd, sl1, K1, psso, K1, k2tog) twice, yfwd, K1, yfwd, sl1, K1, psso, K6.
Row 13: K7, yfwd, sl1, k2tog, psso, yfwd, K1, k2tog, yfwd, K3, yfwd, sl1, K1, psso, K1, yfwd, sl1, k2tog, psso, yfwd, K7.
Row 15: K3, k2tog, yfwd, K1, yfwd, sl1, K1, psso, K2, k2tog, yfwd, K5, yfwd, sl1, K1, psso, K2, k2tog, yfwd, K1, yfwd, sl1, K1, psso, K3.
Row 17: K4, yfwd, sl1, k2tog, psso, yfwd, K4, yfwd, sl1, K1, psso, K3, k2tog, yfwd, K4, yfwd, sl1, k2tog, psso, yfwd, K4.

Row 19: K6, k2tog, (yfwd, K1) twice, sl1, K1, psso, yfwd, sl1, K1, psso, K1, k2tog, yfwd, k2tog, (K1, yfwd) twice, sl1, K1, psso, K6.

Row: 21: K7, (yfwd, sl1, k2tog, psso, yfwd, K3) 3 times, K4.

Row 23: As Row 7.

Row 25: As Row 9.

Row 27: As Row 3.

Row 29: As Row 5.

Row 30: As Row 2.

Repeat Rows 1-30 twice more, then rows 1-22, ending with RS facing.

Row 23: Knit.

Row 24: K3, P23, K3.

With RS facing, cast off loosely.

FINISHING

Lay flat and gently steam to open up lace pattern. Using mattress stitch, join cast-on to cast-off edge.

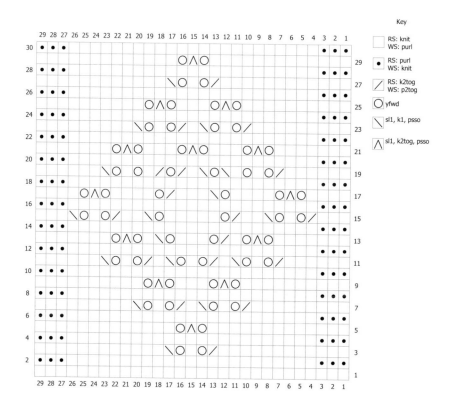

Key

□	RS: knit WS: purl
•	RS: purl WS: knit
╱	RS: k2tog WS: p2tog
○	yfwd
╲	sl1, k1, psso
⋀	sl1, k2tog, psso

Alpine Throw
ROWAN BRUSHED FLEECE

Alpine Throw

Snuggle up on chilly nights under this light as feather, super cosy throw.

TENSION
13 sts and 20 rows to 10cm measured over st st on 6mm (US 11) needles

SIZE
88 cm x 110 cm

INSTRUCTIONS
Using 6mm circular needle and Yarn A, cast on 115 sts.
Knit 6 rows.
Next Row (RS): Knit.
Next Row (WS): K6, P103, K6.
These two rows set the pattern of st st with g st borders.
Repeat these last two rows 6 times more.
Next Row: K6, work 103 sts from chart (using intarsia method) and working the repeat section within the red border twice, K6.
This row sets position of chart. Continue working in this way, maintaining the g st border at each end, until chart is complete.
Work 14 rows in st st with g st borders.
**Knit 6 rows.
Work 50 rows in st st with g st borders. **
Rep from ** to ** once more.
Knit 6 rows.

YOU WILL NEED;

YARN
Rowan Brushed Fleece
A Crag 253
6 x 50g
B Cove 251
1 x 50g

NEEDLES
6mm (No 4) (US 10) circular needle, 80cm long

1 pair 8mm (No 0) (US 11) needles (used for casting off only)

Note: The throw is worked flat, but circular needles are recommended in order to accommodate the large size of the throw.

Work 14 rows in st st with g st borders.
Work 22 rows from chart as before, but
turn the chart upside down and work
rows 22 to 1 so that the two ends of the
throw will be a mirror image.
Work 14 rows in st st with g st borders.
Knit 6 rows
With RS facing and using 8mm (US 11)
needles, cast off loosely.

FINISHING
Sew in all ends neatly on reverse.
Steam gently to finish.

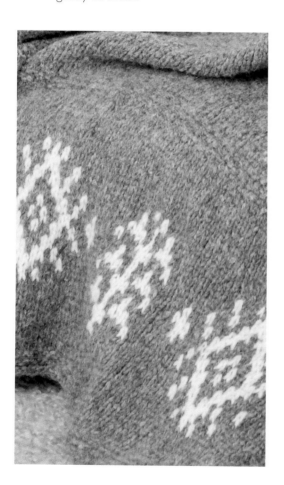

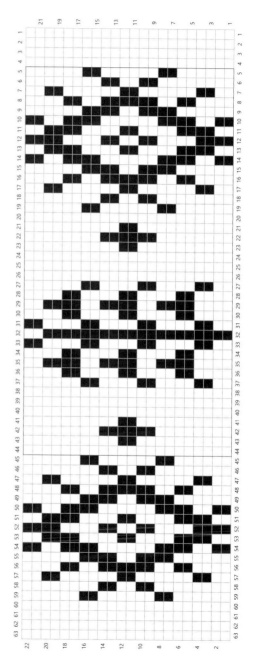

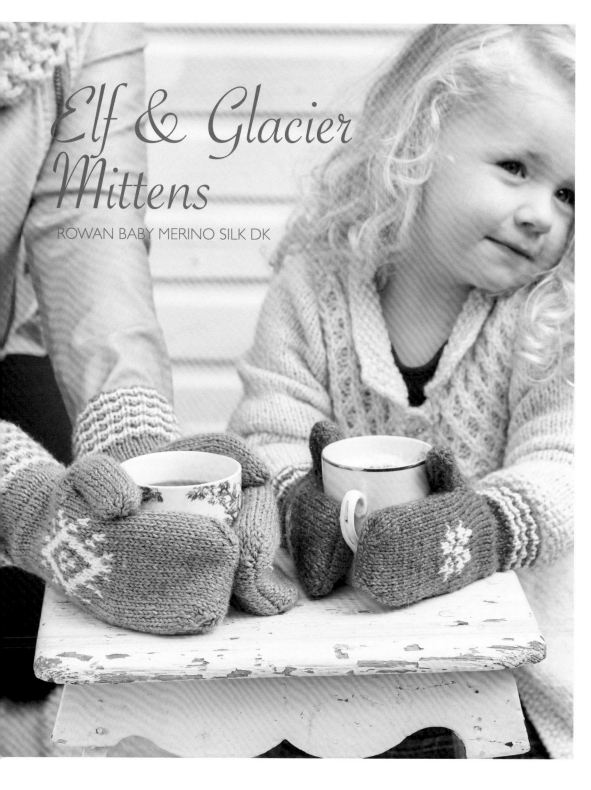

Elf & Glacier Mittens

ROWAN BABY MERINO SILK DK

Elf & Glacier Mittens

We're smitten with mittens - for the young and forever young feel nostalgic in these lovely winter warmers.

TENSION
24 sts and 36 rows to 10cm measured over st st

SIZE
Elf mitten (child age 3-4 years):
17 from wrist to tip
14cm circumference

Glacier mitten (adults):
28cm from wrist to tip
18cm circumference around wrist

Note: for Glacier mittens follow stitches and measurements within brackets.

INSTRUCTIONS
Right Mitten
Using A and 3.75mm (US 3) needles and yarn A, cast on 32 (44) sts.
**Rows 1-2: *K1, P1, rep from * to end.
Change to yarn B.
Rep Rows 1-2.
Change to yarn A.
Taking yarn up the side of work, rep from **, twice (4 times) more.
Continue in yarn A for remainder of mitten.
Work 2 (8) rows in st st.

YOU WILL NEED;

YARN
Rowan Baby Merino Silk DK
A Teal 677 (adult version) or
Strawberry 687 (child's version)
1 x 50g

B Snowdrop 670
1 x 50g

NEEDLES
1 pair 3.75mm (No 10)
(US 3) needles

OTHER SUPPLIES
2 stitch markers
Darning needle

THUMB GUSSET

Row 1: K 16 (22), place stitch marker, M1, K1, M1, place stitch marker, K13 (19). 34 (46) sts.
Row 2: Purl.
Row 3: Knit.
Row 4: Purl.
Row 5: K16 (22), slip first marker, M1, K to second marker, M1, slip second marker, K13 (19). 2 sts inc'd.
Rep the last 4 rows 2 (4) more times, removing markers on last row. 40 (56) sts.
Work 3 (1) rows in st st without shaping.

THUMB

Next Row (RS): K27 (37), turn and cast on 2 sts.
Next Row: P12 (16), turn and cast on 2 sts.
***Continue working on these 14 (18) sts only until thumb measures 2.5 (5)cm ending after a WS row.
Next Row: K1, (K2, k2tog) 3 (4) times, K1. 11 (14) sts.
Next Row: Purl.
Next Row: (K2tog) 5 times, K1 (4). 6 (9) sts.
Break yarn and thread through remaining sts, draw up and fasten off securely, then sew up thumb seam.
With RS facing, rejoin yarn at base of thumb, pick up and knit 4 sts at base of thumb and knit to end of row. 34 (46) sts.
Continue in st st until work measures 8 (11) cm from last thumb gusset row, finishing after a WS row.

SHAPE TOP

Row 1 (RS): K2, *sl1, K1, psso, K10 (16), k2tog, K2, rep from * twice.
Row 2: Purl.

Row 3: K2, *sl1, K1, psso, K8 (14), k2tog, K2, rep from * twice.
Row 4: Purl.
Row 5: K2 *sl1, K1, psso, K6 (12), k2tog, K2, rep from * twice.
Row 6: Purl.
Cast off.

LEFT MITTEN

Work as for Right Mitten until thumb gusset. Proceed as follows;

THUMB GUSSET

Row 1: K13 (19), place stitch marker, M1, K1, M 1, place stitch marker, K16 (22). 34 (46) sts.
Row 2: Purl.
Row 3: Knit.
Row 4: Purl.
Row 5: K13 (19), slip first marker, M1, K to second marker, M1, slip second marker, K16 (22). 2 sts inc'd.
Rep the last 4 rows 2 (4) more times, removing markers on last row. 40 (56) sts.
Work 3 (1) rows in st st without shaping.

THUMB

Knit 24 (34), turn and cast on 2 sts.
Purl 12 (16), turn and cast on 2 sts.

Complete as for Right Mitten from ***

FINISHING

With Yarn B and using charts from Chamonix cushion, use darning needle to add motifs motifs to centre top side of mittens, using the Swiss Darning (aka duplicate stitch) method.

Myrtle
Tea Cosy

ROWAN HANDKNIT COTTON

Myrtle Tea Cosy

Keep your tea toasty too with this simple fair isle knit.

TENSION
20 sts and 28 rows to 10cm measured over st st on 4mm (US 6) needles

MEASUREMENTS
Circumference: 46cm
Height: 21cm

INSTRUCTIONS
Front & Back - Make 2
Using 4mm (US 6) needles and yarn A, cast on 48 sts.
Rows 1-8 (Rib): *K2, P2, rep from * to end.
**Change to yarn B.
Work 4 rows in st st.
Change to yarn A.
Work 2 rows in st st.
Work 7 rows from chart.

Tip: Carry main colour always on top and contrast colour always underneath to avoid twisting yarn.

With Yarn A Purl 1 row.
Repeat from ** once more.
Change to yarn B.
Next Row (RS, dec): *K2tog, K6, rep from * to end.
42 sts.

YOU WILL NEED;

YARN
Rowan Handknit Cotton
A Ice Water 239
1 x 50g
B Ecru 251
1 x 50g
C Linen 205
1 x 50g

NEEDLES
1 pair 4mm (No 8)
(US 6) needles

OTHER SUPPLIES
Darning needle
2 small stitch holders

Next Row: Purl.
Next Row: Knit.
Next Row (WS, dec): *P5, p2tog, rep from * to end. 36 sts.
Change to yarn A.
Next Row: Knit.
Next Row: Purl.
Next Row (RS, dec): *K4, k2tog, rep from * to end. 30 sts.
Next Row: Purl.
Next Row (RS, dec): *K2tog, K3, rep from* to end. 24 sts.
Next Row: Purl.
Next Row (RS, dec): *K2tog, K2, rep from * to end. 18 sts.
Next Row: Purl.
Next Row: *K2tog, K1, rep from * to end. 12 sts.
Leaving about 30cm break yarn and leave sts on stitch holder.

FINISHING
Sew in ends.
With RS together and using mattress stitch, sew the side seams of the tea cosy, leaving a gap at each side for the handle and spout.
Thread a needle with Yarn A and draw through all stitches left on stitch holders. Pull tight to fasten, leaving a small hole for the pompom, and secure yarn ends on WS.

SHAGGY POMPOM
Using yarn B and 4mm (US 6) needles, cast on 20 sts leaving a long tail for sewing up.
Row 1: Cast off 16 sts, K4. 4 sts.
Row 2: K4, turn, cast on 16 sts using cable cast on method. 20 sts.

Repeat these two rows 19 times, then work Row 1, once more.
Cast off.

FINISHING
Starting at cast-on edge, roll up strip to make pompom, and use tail yarn to sew up and secure as you go. Attach to top of tea cosy through hole at the top.

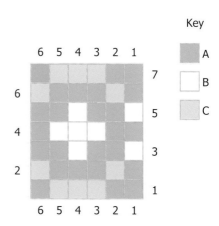

Linda's Luscious Lemon Curd

Linda's Luscious Lemon Curd

This luscious curd is lovely on toast, crumpets, as a cake filling or for a lemony twist spread on some sultana scones.

Makes about 1.15 kg

For a tangier alternative you can replace two of the lemons zest and juice with four limes zest and juice. Finely grate the zest of the lemons, cut in half and squeeze the juice and strain into a measuring jug until there is 300 ml.

Cut the butter into small cubes, put them in a large glass bowl along with the sugar zest and juice, set over a pan of simmering water making sure the water does not boil too rapidly or boil dry, ensuring that the bottom of the bowl does not touch the water. Stir the mixture until all the butter has melted and the sugar has dissolved.

Lightly beat the eggs and the extra yolks in a bowl, but do not whisk them. Then gradually add the beaten eggs to the lemony mixture continually stirring as you go. The mixture will eventually thicken, although it will take about 25mins. Continue until the mixture coats the back of a wooden spoon.

Remove the bowl carefully from the pan and set aside, then ladle the lemony curd into clean sterilized jars and allow to cool. When the curd has cooled, place lids on the jars firmly, label and store in the fridge.

YOU WILL NEED;

6-8 juicy large lemons
570g caser sugar
225g unsalted butter
5 large eggs (plus 2 yokes)

Note: store in fridge and use within 1 month of making.

Mimosa
Jam Pot Covers

ROWAN HANDKNIT COTTON

Mimosa Jam Pot Covers

Give a pretty hand made finish to your home made preserves.

TENSION
24 sts and 29 rows to 10cm measured over st st on 2.75mm (US 5) needles

SIZE
16cm diameter

SPECIAL ABBREVIATIONS
Ssk - slip 1, slip1, knit 2 slip stitches tog through back loop
Yon - yarn over needle to make stitch

INSTRUCTIONS
Using 3.75mm (US 5) needles, cast on 96 sts and divide evenly over 4 needles. 24 sts on each.
Join to work in the round, taking care not to twist sts.
Place marker to denote end of rnd.
Rnd 1: Purl.
Rnd 2: (K5, ssk, K5) 8 times. 88 sts.
Rnd 3: Purl.
Rnd 4: Knit.
Rnd 5: Purl.
Rnd 6: (K4, ssk, K5) 8 times. 80 sts.
Rnd 7 (eyelet Rnd): *K2tog, yon, rep from * to end.
Rnd 8: (K4, ssk, K4) 8 times. 72 sts.
Rnd 9: Knit.
Rnd 10: (K3, ssk, K4) 8 times. 64 sts.

YOU WILL NEED;

YARN
Rowan Handknit Cotton
Ecru 251 or Linen 205
1 x 50g

NEEDLES
Set of 5 double-pointed 3.75mm
(No 9) (US 5) needles

OTHER SUPPLIES
50cm of lace or ribbon per jar
Stitch marker

Rnd 11: Knit.
Rnd 12: (K3, ssk, K3) 8 times. 56 sts.
Rnd 13: Knit.
Rnd 14: (K2, ssk, K3) 8 times. 48 sts.
Rnd 15: Knit.
Rnd 16: (K2, ssk, K2) 8 times. 40 sts.
Rnd 17 (eyelet rnd): As Rnd 7.
Rnd 18: (K1, ssk, K2) 8 times. 32 sts.
Rnd 19: Knit.
Rnd 20: (K1, ssk, K1) 8 times. 24 sts.
Rnd 21: Knit.
Rnd 22: (Ssk, K1) 8 times. 16 sts.
Rnd 23: (Ssk) 8 times. 8 sts.

FINISHING
Break yarn leaving a long tail (30cm) and
using a tapestry needle, thread yarn back
through remaining stitches on needle.
Draw up tightly and secure on WS.
Place on top of jar and tie ribbon or lace
around lid.

Rhubarb & Lime Jam

Rhubarb
and
Lime

Rhubarb
and
Lime

Rhubarb & Lime Jam

Just as delicious on morning toast as teatime scones. Also goes rather well with ginger biscuits or spread on homemade ginger cake.

Makes about 1.3kg

Cut the rhubarb diagonally into short lengths and place in a large ceramic bowl with the other ingredients. Give it a good stir, cover and leave to macerate overnight.

Pour the fruit and sugary juices into a preserving pan and stir over a low heat to dissolve the sugar. Once the sugar has completely dissolved, bring to the boil and continue to cook until the rhubarb is tender and setting point is reached – about 10-15 mins. Skim if necessary.

Tip - To test for setting point; dip a wooden spoon in the pan and hold a spoonful of the jam mixture above it, if strands form that hang from the spoon it is ready. If not continue boiling for another 5 minutes and test again.

Remove the pan from the heat and let it cool for a couple of minutes before pouring the jam into sterilised jars. Seal jars immediately and label and date when cold.

YOU WILL NEED;

1kg rhubarb, trimmed weight
850g golden unrefined granulated sugar
Zest and juice of three limes (oranges can also be substituted)

Heidi Scarf
& Chalet Snood

ROWAN ALPACA CHUNKY

Heidi Scarf

This one row pattern is quick to knit, but gives a fabulous effect.

TENSION
9.5 sts and 14 rows to 10cm measured over patt on 10mm (US 15) needles

SIZE
Width: 17cm
Length: 160cm

INSTRUCTIONS
Using 10mm (US 15) needles and leaving a tail of about 10cm, cast on 20sts.
Row 1: Sl 1 *P1, yrn, p2tog, rep from * to last st, K into back of last st.
Repeat this row until nearly all of yarn is used up, leaving at least 80cm of yarn to cast off and sew in .
Cast off.

**With a large a large-eyed wool needle and tail yarn, make a running stitch along cast-on edge. Pull yarn to gather. Attach BonPom securely.
Rep from ** for cast-off edge.

YOU WILL NEED;

YARN
Rowan Alpaca Chunky
Pigeon 073
2 x 100g

NEEDLES
1 pair 10mm (No 000)
(US 15) needles

OTHER SUPPLIES
2 x Twilleys Faux Fur Bonpom,
Mink 002
Large-eyed wool needle

Chalet Snood

Why not try a snood in the same pattern but a different colour?

YOU WILL NEED;

YARN
Rowan Alpaca Chunky
Dove 070
2 x 100g

NEEDLES
1 pair 10mm (No 000)
(US 15) needles

TENSION
9.5 sts and 14 rows to 10cm measured over patt on 10mm (US 15) needles

MEASUREMENTS
Depth: 36cm
Circumference: 75cm

INSTRUCTIONS
Using 10mm (US 15) needles, cast on 35 sts.
Row 1: Sl 1 *P1, yrn, p2tog, rep from * to last st, K into back of last st.
Repeat this row until work measures approx 75cm.
Cast off.

FINISHING
Sew cast-on and cast-off edges together.

Crocus & Petal Scarflette

ROWAN BABY MERINO
SILK DK OR ROWAN
KIDSILK HAZE

Crocus & Petal Scarflette

A pretty perfect little neck warmer.

TENSION
28 sts and 26 rows to 10cm measured over patt on 4mm (US 6) needles with Kidsilk Haze held double

SIZE
One size
Width: 18cm
Length: 110cm

INSTRUCTIONS
CROCUS SCARFLETTE
Using 4mm (US 6) needles cast on 51 sts.
Row 1: K1, *yfwd, K3, k3tog, K3, yfwd, K1, rep from *
to end.
Row 2: Knit.
Rep Rows 1-2 until work measures approx 110cm ending on a knit row, leaving at least 60cm of yarn for casting off.
Cast off loosely.

PETAL SCARFLETTE
Using 4mm (US 6) needles and with **yarn held double**, cast on 51 sts and follow pattern as for Crocus Scarflette.

FINISHING
Pin work flat and steam lightly to open up lace pattern.
Sew in ends.

YOU WILL NEED;

YARN
*Rowan Baby Merino Silk DK
(Crocus Scarflette)
Strawberry 687
2 x 50g*

*Rowan Kidsilk Haze
(Petal Scarflette)
Grace 580
2 x 25g*

NEEDLES
*1 pair 4mm (No 8)
(US 6) needles*

Meribel Poncho

ROWAN ALPACA CHUNKY

Meribel Poncho

Wrap yourself up in this luxurious alpaca poncho, for the most stylish cover up of the season.

TENSION
11 sts and 14 rows to 10cm measured over patt on 10mm (US 15) needles

SIZE
Each piece (before sewing up)
Length: 91cm
Width: 63cm

ABBREVIATIONS
C4B: Slip 2 sts onto cable needle and hold in back, K2 from LH needle, K2 from cable needle.
C4F: Slip 2 sts onto cable needle and hold in front, K2 from LH needle, K2 from cable needle.

INSTRUCTIONS
Make 2 rectangles as follows;
Using 10mm (US 15) needles, cast on 70 sts.
Knit 4 rows.
Row 1: K12, P2, K8, P2, K22, P2, K8, P2, K12.
Row 2: K4, P8, K2, P8, K2, P22, K2, P8, K2, P8, K4.
Row 3: K12, P2, C4B, C4F, P2, K22, P2, C4B, C4F, P2, K12.
Row 4: As Row 2.
Rep Rows 1-4 until work measures approx 89cm (approx 30 pattern repeats).

YOU WILL NEED;

YARN
Rowan Alpaca Chunky
Dove 070
10 x 100g

NEEDLES
1 pair 10mm (No 000) (US 15)

OTHER SUPPLIES
Large crochet hook for tassels

Knit 4 rows.
Cast off.

FINISHING
Lay both pieces flat and steam gently.
Using the diagram as a guide, sew the
poncho together.

Make tassels using 3 lengths of yarn
11cm long. Using a large crochet hook,
place at intervals all the way round
bottom edge of poncho.

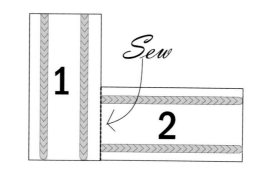

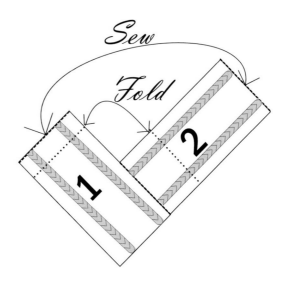

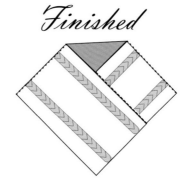

Igloo Socks

ROWAN COCOON

Igloo Socks

Spoil your feet in these toasty slipper socks.
Perfect for lounging.

TENSION
15 sts and 19 rows to 10cm measured over st st on
6mm (US 10 1/2) needles

SIZE
One size - large (fits up to size 10 foot)
Leg length (with cuff folded): 18cm
Length of sock from heel to toe: 28cm
Length can be adjusted by working more or fewer
rows in the foot section before working the toe.

SPECIAL INSTRUCTIONS: WRAP STITCHES
Work the wrap stitch on a knit row as follows:
1. Work up to the 'turn', with the yarn to the back
of the work, slip the stitch purlwise onto the
right-hand needle.

2. Bring the yarn forward between the two needles so
that it is sitting at the front of the work.

3. Slip the same stitch back onto the left-hand needle
and take the yarn back between the two needles. Turn
the work. One stitch is wrapped and you are ready to
continue the next row.

Work wrap stitch on a purl row as follows:
1. Work up to the 'turn' and keep yarn to the front of
the work, slip the next stitch purlwise onto the right-
hand needle.

YOU WILL NEED;

YARN
Rowan Cocoon
Shown in Moon 836, Alpine
802, Polar 801, Frost 806
and Calisto 842
2 x 100g

NEEDLES
1 pair 6mm (No 3)
(US 10 1/2) needles

OTHER SUPPLIES
2 removable/lockable
stitch markers

2. Move the yarn to the back of the work between the two needles.

3. Slip the same stitch back onto the left-hand needle and take the yarn back between the two needles. Turn the work. One stitch is wrapped and you are ready to continue the next row.

INSTRUCTIONS
Using 6mm (US 10 1/2) needles, cast on 40 sts.
Work K2, P2 rib until work measures 18cm from cast on edge.
Cont in st st until work measures 27cm, finishing after a WS row.

HEEL SHAPING
The heel is worked in short rows as follows;
Following the next 70 rows of wrap stitch pattern
Row 1: K13, wrap next stitch, turn.
Row 2 and all following WS rows: Purl
Row 3: K12, wrap next stitch, turn.
Row 5: K11, wrap next stitch, turn.
Row 7: K10, wrap next stitch, turn.
Row 9: K9, wrap next stitch, turn.
Row 11: K8, wrap next stitch, turn.
Row 13: K7, wrap next stitch, turn.
Row 15: K6, wrap next stitch, turn.
Row 17: K5, wrap next stitch, turn.
Row 19: K6, wrap next stitch, turn.
Row 21: K7, wrap next stitch, turn.
Row 23: K8, wrap next stitch, turn.
Row 25: K9, wrap next stitch, turn.
Row 27: K10, wrap next stitch, turn.
Row 29: K11, wrap next stitch, turn.
Row 31: K12, wrap next stitch, turn.
Row 33: K13, wrap next stitch, turn.
Row 35: Knit across ALL stitches
Row 36: P13, wrap next stitch, turn.
Row 37 and all following RS rows: Knit.
Row 38: P12, wrap next stitch, turn.
Row 40: P11, wrap next stitch, turn.
Row 42: P10, wrap next stitch, turn.

Row 44: P9, wrap next stitch, turn.
Row 46: P8, wrap next stitch, turn.
Row 48: P7, wrap next stitch, turn.
Row 50: P6, wrap next stitch, turn.
Row 52: P5, wrap next stitch, turn.
Row 54: P6, wrap next stitch, turn.
Row 56: P7, wrap next stitch, turn.
Row 58: P8, wrap next stitch, turn.
Row 60: P9, wrap next stitch, turn.
Row 62: P10, wrap next stitch, turn.
Row 64: P11, wrap next stitch, turn.
Row 66: P12, wrap next stitch, turn.
Row 68: P13, wrap next stitch, turn.
Row 70: Purl across ALL stitches and place marker at each end of row.
Beg with a RS row, work in st st until work measures 15cm or desired length from markers.

SHAPE TOE
Row 1 (RS): K7, k2tog, K2, k2tog tbl, K14, k2tog, K2, k2tog tbl, K7. 36 sts
Row 2 and all following WS rows: Purl.
Row 3: K6, k2tog, K2, k2tog tbl, K12, k2tog, K2, k2tog tbl, K6. 32 sts
Row 5: K5, k2tog, K2, k2tog tbl, K10, k2tog, K2, k2tog tbl, K5. 28 sts
Row 7: K4, k2tog, K2, k2tog tbl, K8, k2tog, K2, k2tog tbl, K4. 24 sts
Row 9: K3, k2tog, K2, k2tog tbl, K6, k2tog, K2, k2tog tbl, K3. 20 sts
Row 11: K2, k2tog, K2, k2tog tbl, K4 k2tog, K2, k2tog tbl, K2. 16 sts
Row 12: Purl.
Cast off.

FINISHING
Lay work flat and gently steam. Do not press rib. Using mattress stitch sew up from the toe end along long side of sock but reversing the seam at the turnover part of the rib, turn the sock inside out and carefully backstitch across toe seam, slightly tapering for left and right foot.

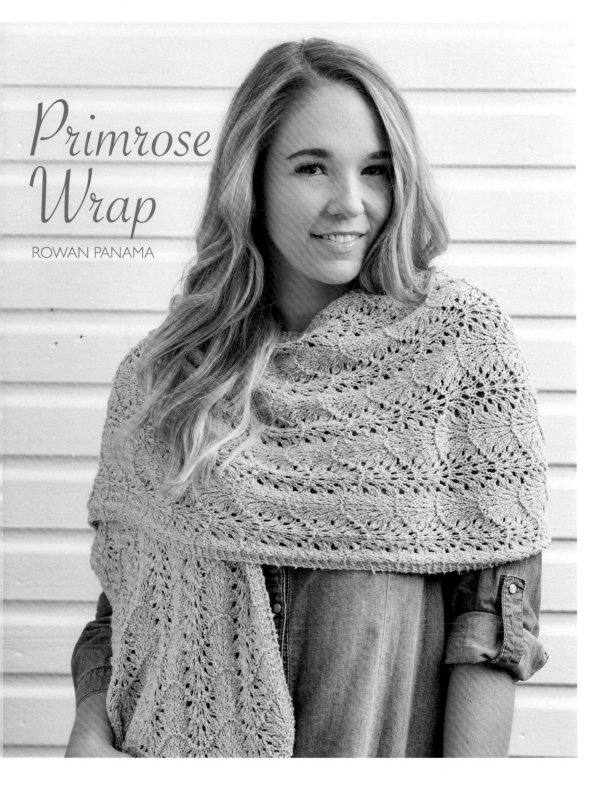

Primrose
Wrap

ROWAN PANAMA

Primrose Wrap

Elegant, shale pashmina in this delightful cotton/linen mix to give the most beautiful drape.

YOU WILL NEED;

YARN
Rowan Panama
Orchid 304
5 X 50g

NEEDLES
1 pair 4mm (No 8)
(US 6) needles

TENSION
28 sts and 25 rows to 10cm measured over pattern on 4mm (US 6) needles

SIZE
Width: 35cm
Length: 168cm

INSTRUCTIONS
Note: There is a 4 stitch knit border at each end of every row.

Using 4mm (US 6) needles, cast on 98 sts.
Knit 4 rows.
Work from chart or written instructions as follows;
Row 1: Knit
Row 2: K4, purl to last 4sts, K4
Row 3 (pattern row): K4, (k2tog) 3 times, *(yfwd, K1) 6 times, (k2tog) 6 times, rep from * 4 times, (yfwd, K1) 6 times, (k2tog) 3 times, K4.
Row 4: As Row 2. The yfwd sts from the previous row should be purled.
Row 5: As Row 1.
Row 6: As Row 2.
Row 7: As Row 3.
Row 8: As Row 2.

Row 9: As Row 1.
Row 10: As Row 2.
Row 11: As Row 3.
Row 12: Knit. The yfwd sts from the previous row should be worked as knit sts. Rep Rows 1-12 until work measures approximately 165cm ending on row 12 (34 pattern repeats).
Knit 4 rows.
Cast off loosely.

FINISHING
Sew in ends and press lightly if necessary.

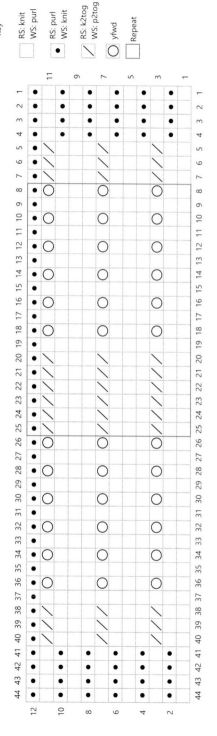

Key

RS: knit WS: purl	RS: purl WS: knit	RS: k2tog WS: p2tog	yfwd	Repeat

Cheese Scones

Cheese Scones

We serve these scones freshly made every Wednesday afternoon at Jolie with a knit and cream tea. They are so popular our customers usually skip lunch.

Makes a baker's dozen using a 2 inch cutter.

Heat oven to 180 degrees.

Double sieve the flours into a bowl with baking powder and salt. Rub in the butter into until the mixture resembles damp sand.

Add black pepper and cheese - keeping some of the cheese back for topping. Add the beaten egg and a couple of tablespoons of milk if necessary (again leaving a little egg left in the bowl to brush the tops).
Mix well together and knead to blend.
Roll out thickly (about an inch) onto a floured surface.
Cut out and place on a baking tray.
Brush with remaining egg and top with leftover cheese mixture and extra black pepper.
Bake in oven for 10 mins.

Serve immediately with lashings of cold butter.

YOU WILL NEED;

25g unsalted butter
110g Self Raising flour
110g Plain flour
1 tsp baking powder
Pinch salt
2 eggs, beaten
450g finely grated cheeses of your choice. I always include Gruyere and an extra mature cheddar. A smoked cheese works well and of course Parmesan is good.
Cracked black pepper.

Alabama Slammer

Alabama Slammer

Get in the mood and enjoy a throwback cocktail whilst keeping warm on winter nights.

Fill a tall glass with ice and pour over equal measures (35ml) of amaretto Di Saronno, Southern Comfort and home made sloe gin. Give a good stir and top up with freshly squeezed orange juice. Add a slice of orange. Cheers!

YOU WILL NEED;

35ml Amaretto Di Saronno
(or any Amaretto)
35ml Southern Comfort
(Whiskey based liqueur)
35ml Sloe Gin
(Sloe berry infused gin)
70ml Freshly squeezed orange juice
Slice of orange

Abbreviations

K	knit
P	purl
st(s)	stitch(es)
inc	increas(e)(ing)
dec	decreas(e)(ing)
st st	stocking stitch (1 row K, 1 row P)
g st	garter stitch (K every row)
beg	begin(ning)
foll	following
rem	remain(ing)
rev st st	reverse stocking stitch (1 row K , 1 row P)
rep	repeat
alt	alternate
cont	continue
patt	pattern
tog	together
mm	millimetres
cm	centimetres
in(s)	inch(es)
RS	right side
WS	wrong side
sl 1	slip one stitch
psso	pass slipped stitch over
p2sso	pass 2 slipped stitches over
tbl	through back of loop
M1	make one stitch by picking up horizontal loop before next stitch and knitting into back of it
M1P	make one stitch by picking up horizontal loop before next stitch and purling into back of it
yfwd	yarn forward
yrn	yarn round needle
meas	measures
yon	yarn over needle to make stitch
yfrn	yarn forward round needle
wyib	with yarn at back
sl2togK	slip 2 stitches together knitways
Ssk	slip 1, slip1, knit 2 slip stitches tog through back loop

For materials and props used in this
book contact Jolie:
80 High St, Walkern,
Stevenage, SG2 7PG

jolie_walkern@yahoo.co.uk
www.jolie-home.co.uk
01438 861717

Acknowledgements

We would like to thank all our lovely customers who join us regularly for Knit and Chat sessions at our shop - for their support, inspiration and helping with knitting up some of the projects. And of course to Sophie, Esme and Teddy for being such wonderful models.

Special thanks to Sharon Northcott for believing in and encouraging us so much at the start of this project. Thanks also to Sharon Brant and to Darren Brant and the team at Quail Publishing for making this book possible.

We would also like to thank both our families and friends for all their love and continued support.

Dany & Linda